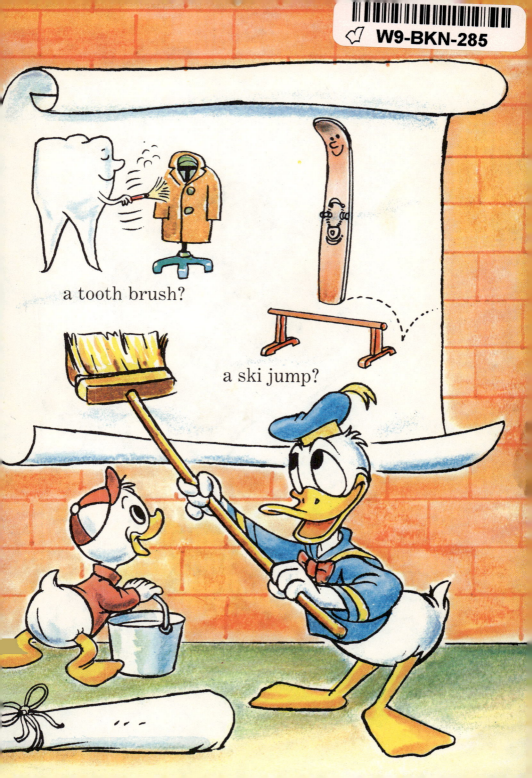

a tooth brush?

a ski jump?

BOOK CLUB EDITION

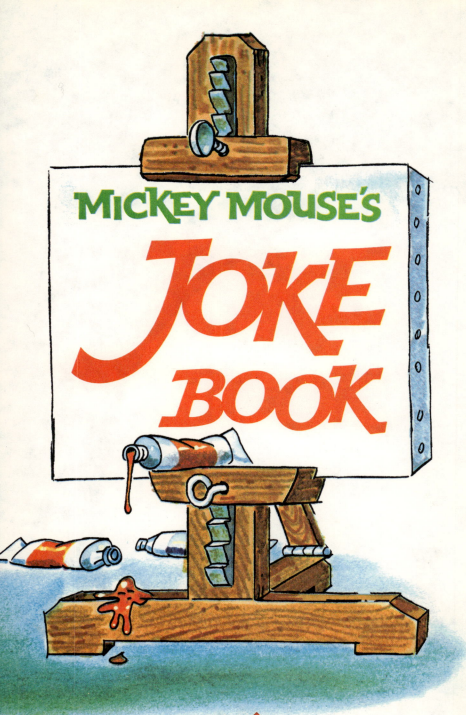

MICKEY MOUSE'S JOKE BOOK

Random House 🏠 New York

Library of Congress Cataloging in Publication Data
Mickey Mouse's joke book.
(Disney's wonderful world of reading)
An easy-to-read collection of jokes including such Disney characters as Goofy, Donald Duck
and Mickey Mouse.
[1. Joke books]   PZ8.7.M47   [E]   73-393
ISBN 0-394-82632-9   ISBN 0-394-92632-3 (GLB)
Manufactured in the United States of America

D E F G H I J K
6 7 8 9
B

"I sure am glad I'm not a bird, Mickey."

"Why, Goofy?"

"Because I cannot fly."

"You sure grow a lot of peaches here,"
Mickey said to the farmer.

"We sure do," the farmer answered.
"What do you do with all of them?" asked Mickey.
"We eat what we can," said the farmer.

"And what we can't
...we can!"

"Donald, why is Goofy
holding the mirror
when his eyes
are closed?"

"He wants to see
what he looks like
when he's asleep."

"Would you give me a quarter, Mickey?
I want to go see my family."

"Where *is* your family, Louie?"

"At the movies!"

"Where are you running, Goofy?"
"To my new job, Mickey."

"Where do you work?"
"At the Eagle Laundry."
"What do you do?"

EAGLE
LAUNDRY

"Wash eagles, of course."

"Hello, Jimmy, I love my new house.
I can see the sun rise from my bed."

"That's nothing, Dick. From *my* bed
I can see the kitchen sink."

"Mickey," asked Jiminy Cricket,
"suppose you found ten cents
in one pants pocket
and twenty cents in the other.
What would you have?"

"Somebody else's pants on."

"Louie, here is a quarter.
How about getting us
two ice cream cones?"

"Please give me
two chocolate
ice cream cones.
One for me and
one for my Uncle Donald."

OOPS!

"I'm sorry, Uncle Donald.
I dropped *your* ice cream cone."

What did the baby porcupine
say to the cactus?

"Is that you, Mama?"

DID
YOU
EVER
SEE...

a horse fly?

UNFAIR

a clock strike?

a pen point?

a window box?

a rabbit punch?

a jelly roll?

a barn dance?

a fish bowl?

"My, my! I never saw a pair of socks like that. Did you?"

"Sure. My brother has a pa[ir] just like them."

Five copy cats are sitting on a wall.

If one jumps off, how many are left?

None!

"Mickey, we found something
so you can see through the wall."
"What do you call it, Louie?"

"A window!"

"Hello, boys," said Mickey.
"Do you like your school?"
"Sometimes," they answered.
"When is that?" Mickey asked.

"When it's closed."

"Why are you crying, Henry?"

"Because my new shoes hurt."

"That's because you put them on the wrong feet."

"Well, they're the only feet I have."

"Do you have any alligator shoes?"

"Yes, ma'am. What size shoes does your alligator wear?"

"Charlie, your story about your dog
is exactly the same as your brother's."

"I know....It's the same dog."

"Mickey, is it true that bears will not hurt you
if you carry a sling shot?"

"That depends on how fast you carry it."

"Donald, how do you like Goofy's car?"

"Not much, Mickey.
Its wheels are gone
and it hasn't any motor.
About all it has is a horn."

"Then how does it go?"

"Honk. Honk."

"It sure rains a lot here.
What do you raise most?...Corn?"

"No! Umbrellas."

"Mrs. Green, your daughter would be
a fine dancer except for two things."

"What are they?"

"Her feet!"

"I'm sorry to hear that Sue Green
will not be able to come to school today.
I hope her cold gets better soon.
Who is this calling?"

"It's my mother."

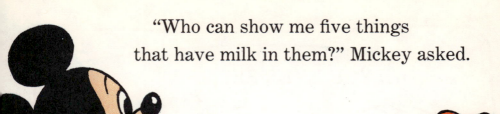

"Who can show me five things
that have milk in them?" Mickey asked.

"I can," said Goofy.

BUTTER   ICE CREAM   CHEESE

TWO COWS

DID YOU EVER SEE...

a clam bake?

a banana peel?